Chanekka Pullens Publishing Presents

MY JOURNALS TO PURPOSE

BY: MICHELLE HOWELL

ISBN: 979-8-218-38420-3

My Journals to Purpose

Published by Chanekka Pullens Publishing

Edited by Chanekka Pullens

Cover art created by Michelle Howell

Books may be purchased in quantity and/or special sales by contacting the author by email at: michellevhowell@gmail.com , with 'Book Purchase' in the subject line.

Printed in the United States of America

I pray this book lands in the hands of a girl who does not feel like a daughter or feels worthy of the call on her life. I pray that you see through me that God uses our stories for His glory.

See you on the other side, sis.

For my family this book is only the introduction of what God is going to do.

Aunt B, this book is a testament of how the word of our testimony can set us free.

And to every girl that believes their story is a bad one to tell, read mine and see how God turned it around for good.

RIP Grandma! You were my inspiration. RIP Grandad! Thanks for LEGACY! RIP Russell. Thank you for believing in me.

Romans 8:28 And we know that all things work together for good to those who love God, who are called according to his purpose

How it started.

Trauma Drama

People always assume married parents equate to a better life, but I disagree. I didn't know I had daddy issues until I recreated his character to my friends at school. Everyone around me had great single moms or grandparents raising them. Honestly, I used to wish that was my storyline growing up. My mother and dad had opposite work shifts for as long as I can remember. My mom worked the second shift, and my dad worked the first shift. The days they were home at the same time were my bad days. I watched my mom get torn down frequently. I eventually got mentally strong and unafraid of my dad for her. I was around the age of thirteen when I began talking back in defense of my mom. She never had my back though, but I knew it was only because she didn't know how. I had enough fight for her and I. My dad couldn't stand me because I knew his truth. All I remember is confronting my dad my entire childhood and never backing down. I knew once graduation came, he was going to make sure I was out of his house.

My dad couldn't stand that I knew things he tried so hard to hide. I honestly believe he was afraid of what I'd do with that knowledge. There was nothing I didn't know that my family could keep away from me. I figured the more I knew, the more I could protect. Even though I didn't feel protected.

My mom was silent my entire childhood. She spoiled my sister and I with material things. I don't recall hugs, kisses, or talks with her. It didn't take away the fact I knew she loved us. As a child, I thought so many unkind things about my mom. When truth be told, she was only doing what she knew. She watched her mother be a good wife by standing by her husband right, wrong, or indifferent. So, I never had any expectations for my mother, as I did my father. I guess because he had power, and she had none. I promised myself I would not be my mother, but that promise led me to only becoming my dad. A loudmouth, inconsiderate, egotistical jerk.

My Hype Man Is Now Gone

The loss of my living parents was only the beginning of my hell. My Uncle Mann was brutally murdered on July 04, 2008. My hype man is now gone, and I am left with nobody to love me unconditionally. I never expressed how his death left me because I never had room until I unpacked some stuff. He was my person. I understood him and he understood me. He made me feel seen and heard, always. He used to be our vacation driver. The last vacation we had with him is the one I remember so well because I punched him in his mouth for disrespecting my mom to impress my dad. God, forgive me! I remember my uncle getting drunk one day and one of my dad's friends knocking him clean off the porch. I immediately approached my dad and his friend in defense of my uncle and got him out of there. My love language was becoming how my dad expressed his.

Not IN Love, But IN Need

I always cared about the guys I dated, but never more than myself. The first guy I ever cared for was my best friend, New New. We met over Myspace, and he attended a different high school than I. He had a girlfriend I discovered after I fell in-like with him. I continued to entertain him until he was incarcerated. I moved on to entertain the idea of a close family friend Snooks. I, yes, I made that situation more than it should have been. He was a guy that made it clear he did not want more with me but went along. I was a virgin, unaffectionate, and filled with trauma in this period of my life so I could understand.

Senior year, my friend since 6th grade, Jerry Berry, tells me, "You shouldn't be crying over no guy." He became the one. No, not the one as in THE ONE, but the one who tolerated me. In my eyes, that was love from what I knew and seen. At age seventeen, we started dating and needing each other to survive. We witnessed each other in all seasons you can think of. Co-dependence at its finest. I just knew he was chosen by God. Unfortunately, our lack of spiritual covering and independence destroyed all positive possibilities for us. We became extremely toxic and unhealthy. He was my family; it was no getting rid of him. He became my air until we had our baby girl in 2014.

Lost In The Sauce

No one ever told me that by having a child, I'd lose a sense of self. In hindsight, it was a good thing because who I had become had to be destroyed. I did everything but call for help from friends, family, and God! I was operating out of brokenness, confusion, and hurt. I knew I wanted and needed more so I began blogging and sharing it with the world. I began discovering myself through the world. I didn't know how to properly heal, feel, or be. I started drinking alcohol, having sex, and trying drugs. I was lost in the sauce. I just wanted out of this dark hole I dug myself in. I was frustrated because I was figuring things out with a child and a man who spiritually didn't get what was happening. At the time, neither did I.

Post-Partum - May 11, 2018

I've always been transparent
Until I became a parent
Shit got real
I began to feel
Feel things I never felt before
I became in touch with so much
more
First time I looked into her eyes
I seen life
A life worth living for
Before her. It was just me
no purpose - just living freely
life was no longer a game
I seen people and things differently
I prayed more
I cried more
I became gay for my friends

Possessive?

I became a jealous bitch behind

closed doors

I never spoke on it because it never

bothered me

Until it bothered me.

I became less friendly

I had to stop tripping and get in

tune with my family

I never fell off

I just fell back

Completely stopped expecting

things

From people and the universe

Because I realized "knowing" is a

curse

So I'd 'sleep' more because I couldn't

stand being awake

I had no real love to give; I felt so fake

Blog 1/5 - December 2018

Today, I walked away from an eight-year relationship with my child's father. I did not walk away because he was anything less than good, but because God said so. Most women in my life would call me stupid. The reason behind this drastic decision is because I stopped putting God first in my life. Why NOW? Trust me, before today, I hesitated because I had legit plans of being this man's wife. God did not let up until he made his point of being 'first'. I noticed I was losing sight NOT knowing at the time it was God's doing. My vision worsened. I was seeing things in a blur. My vision became unclear. Hell, I, who once was a work-a-holic, became a person with a lack of drive. I became dependent on someone other than God financially, emotionally, mentally, etc. I'd do things like create new social accounts, begin new projects impulsively, cut my hair expecting a change within. When the real change needed to come from me. It wasn't until my 25th birthday (4.9.18) that I realized God's light on my life. I found myself constantly rebooting myself because I had lost my true self somewhere in between loving my HS sweetheart and creating a life at twenty-one.

I realized I needed to make an extreme shift sooner rather than later. I'd always say things were good, but they could be better. I never actually knew what I meant until now. I would catch myself adding everything but God to OUR grass for the green-ER effect. It had gotten to a point where I'd be the bad guy all the time because my actions would show I needed or wanted more spiritually. He'd always look at me as if I had insulted him, or act as if I cheated on him. I am now understanding a man that has not yet accepted God fully in his life will not be able to grasp what spiritual warfare is.

This was the beginning of me getting found. The more I shoveled through the dirt, the more I could see clearer. I grew up in church because my grandfather was a preacher. So, I knew I'd be found, I just didn't know when. I've always seen the religion side of God, but not until I got lost did I experience the relationship side of God.

Purpose, Is That You?

As my relationship was evolving with God, I not only was discovering my identity in Christ, but my purpose. I didn't even know what I was doing at the time. I was just doing it.

Blog titled "Purpose" - May 18, 2020

Have you ever felt uncomfortably different? You are not alone, I have too. That there is called purpose. God will continue to shift you until you take notice of the hints he has given you. To make a point God will make everything you do undesirable. God will even make those you love unlovable. You will eventually notice those indicators are signs of God wanting to give you more. These shifts I speak of will make you feel alone, or even crazy. I don't speak on purpose lightly because this is bigger than a job, or a degree. Your purpose is the result and the highest power you'll receive if you are obedient to God. I know many young people think after high school they have it all figured out. Hell, even after college. I am here to tell you to trust those shifts, signs, and feelings. Don't just get the highest paying job, or a degree you may never use just to say you graduated. Dig deep and purpose hunt. I know you are probably thinking, "Are you living in your purpose?" Am I right? I can proudly say, "YES, I AM!" I have certifications in the medical field for many different positions and I am a creator of a brand I am most proud of. Not much, huh? It is to me because I have worked GOOD jobs that made GREAT money but didn't serve my soul. I also am doing things I passionately love doing. It is not a day that goes by that I am upset with my choice of living because I am helping people with their physical and mental health. Most people are afraid to live their purpose due to failure. My baby sister Sarah once told me that "failure only comes from people." In other words, people are only taught failure from other people. Don't let someone else's opinion, or "no likes" dictate your success. Fear is the most common cause of why so many people are not living their purpose and are stuck in positions.

Time to take a leap of faith.

Distracted - May 22, 2020

After a long-term relationship I wanted to explore the other side. So, I did. In 2018 I witnessed "hot girl summer". It was an insightful experience. Each guy taught me something that I not once knew lived inside of me. Don't be confused, their sex only confirmed I wasn't missing anything. It was how they perceived me before exploring me intimately that taught me valuable lessons. Some may say my hot girl summer was only a trial run due to it being short lived, but for me, it was a personal externship to womanhood.

God has a funny way of bringing things full circle. After experience and growth, I've learned to keep minimal distractions and to stay away from anything that does not keep me aligned with my purpose.

Sarah Jakes-Roberts explains full circle as, "a series of developments that lead back to the original source, or position to a complete reversal of the original position." For instance, look at the start date of my blogs below which show May 2018 and the date I started back blogging May 2020. Same vision, same purpose. Just with a whole new understanding and perspective of life, but still intentional of course.

I say this to say I planted a seed and got distracted two summers ago. BUT I am back. Don't let summer distract you from growing YOUR seed. This is the perfect season to grow🌱.

YOU have purpose. Stay clear.

I share this truth because sex was a distraction for me. Hopefully this allows you to "get real" and remove the distractions.

What is keeping YOU from your divine purpose?

Blog 2/5 - February 26, 2021

Dear mom,

Wow, I never thought I'd be here. I never thought I'd experience peace. Not even a slice. I used to be so upset at you, dad, and even God for allowing me to have life. I didn't know how to navigate throughout life with power 27 years ago. The power of being able to see the unseen and feel other people's stuff. I battled with it. I hid from it. Now I have an understanding that 'this' power is a gift. Today, I run WITH it and not from it.

And I know it must've been terrifying to watch me grow

fearlessly in this BIG world without your teaching.

I know you would've taught me if you knew how. <3

I searched for your heart for a long time in this BIG world. While searching for something that may not exist, I found my own heart. And within my heart I found God buried under all my stuff. He saw my lack of and encouraged me to plant new seeds to grow new beginnings. So, I did. Those new beginnings have bloomed. (Me being one of them.) I know I don't always say or do the right things. But know that I know your heart and I know where it is NOW. Buried. Set yourself free, mama. You deserve to smile again. You deserve to heal and feel good stuff. I want you to cry out to God and say everything you can't fix your lips to say to me – to Him. Let Him remove your stresses. Let Him be confident in your purpose here on earth. Trust me it is more than being a mom, wife, daughter, and sister. Be open to love from your daughters. Find your heart and make it visible. Unbury God. Allow light and peace in your life.

January 26, 2021

Prayer: Dear God, today I woke up early as usual by the spirit. I am certain God has something BIG in store. I'm preparing for it. I have clarity and vision. I'm hungry. I'm determined. I used to feel crazy, but now I am certain in his plan. When you are carrying purpose, you can't just handle it any kind of way. You must talk to God about the small and big details. He wants in. I'd be vein if I was to say this vision is my own, for he created me. I've been implementing better habits in my life consistently and I love it. I pray it remains. I am being the change I want to be and see. In Jesus name, Amen.

Pastor SJR Notes

Just because something stimulates your revelation, that does not mean act impulsively. Let your now develop your "purpose". You are anointed. God is increasing you. Continue preparing. God will push you out in due time when you are ready. You must be obedient in your now for God to trust you with your next. Humble yourself, so that you are focused on your now. Your next just happens. Your reality will soon support your revelation.

Submit to it now. You're going to need maturity and wisdom. Your now is developing you. The good and the bad.

Prayer: Dear God, I'm sorry I didn't trust you and for even believing you gave up on me. Now I see you've been creating a better me for purpose. Thank you. I love you father! In Jesus name, Amen.

January 30, 2021

Prayer: Dear God, I come to you today with a thankful heart. I've been through a lot but somehow, I still look to you in hopes of something good. I know not all bad is to hurt me. Romans 8:28 – "And we know that God causes all things to work together for good to those who love God, to those who are called according to His purpose." The bad has taught me more valuable lessons than the good. I don't trust anymore. Those days of being naïve are over. I trust you more than ever, Lord. I will continue to pray to you, Lord. I need to break the habit of being a perfectionist and just be. In this season, Lord, I am applying all lessons and staying focused on you. As Sarah Jakes said, "I want to submit to my now." So, when my next happens. Happens! I ask for you to continue ordering my steps. In Jesus name, Amen.

January 31, 2021

Pastor SJR "Taking Form" Sermon Notes

Yesterday's devotion was right on time. Every day I am receiving confirmation that everything that is happening is supposed to. I am anointed. My life is God's. I am taking form. This part of my story is more of God and less of me. I can no longer make decisions without God's confirmation. God wants to know can you still lead even when going through a split. God wants you to know you still have the oil. If you are still greasy, God reveals himself in the breaking. 2020 was the year of breaking for sure! God wants you to reign on your domain. God wants you to control your emotions because you have influence. You are a king. Don't change who you are. Change your atmosphere and you will become.

February 1, 2021

Pastor SJR "End Of An Era"

Sermon Notes

When an era ends a new beginning emerges. I finally found my sound. My now may not match my revelation, but I know it will in this new era. Let me be obedient to my now. Surrender to God's teaching. Surrender to now; increase! Surrender to God's pace and not my own. Just because I'm held back now does not mean I'm not preparing. I am preparing for the moment when I will be in it. My perspective has changed about my anointing. That is why my circle and activities have changed. Now I am protecting my oil. Example: Mom, I know you have issues, but I must protect my oil. That is why I can be alone. I will not miss my moment! Your moment will be disguised as a problem. Be who God called you to be. The breakthrough is in the problem. Take authority over the problem. Don't let it take authority over your household. Who would you be if you took authority over the problems in your life? This version has always been in me, but I didn't have the right components: circle, vision, and favor. "The two most important days in your life will be when you are born and when you find out why you were born." -Mark Twain

Prayer: Dear God, I will step into my why all the way. I am gifted. It is okay for an era to end. I trust you, Lord! In Jesus name, Amen.

<u>February 5, 2021</u>

Prayer: Dear God, I come to you today asking for guidance and strength. I've been feeling good, very hopeful. I must say I am grateful to have purpose and vision. Things seem much clearer on this side. I have been wrestling with you for a long time. I always wanted my parents to see me for who I am and love who I am. But I am learning what people do not understand is based off their comprehension. So, I am thankful for those who try to understand. I know a lot of people feel I folded since I went missing in action, but I don't care because for once, I must do the work to get closer to you. I am a leader. I am learning how to listen, work, and communicate to and with you only. No more outside noise. I will stay working and preparing until my purpose is ready. I will wait for your okay. God continue working on me. In Jesus name, Amen.

February 6, 2021

Prayer: Dear God, I come to you today for patience. I want my attitude towards the things and people I find difficult to be treated kindly. I don't want to miss the joy or lesson by being frustrated. God, keep working on me. I see what you are doing inside of me, and I like it. I am so thankful for purpose. God, you are amazing. You took broken me and healed me. The man, or the friend I will have in the future will respect me because I now respect myself. I will no longer tolerate anything less because I will become my best self. The few relationships I have I am grateful for. The relationships in my family. I am thankful for progress. God, I ask you please to never take your hands off me, or my connections. In Jesus name, Amen.

February 7, 2021

Prayer: Dear God, thank you for everything you've done for me and currently doing. I don't take for granted your grace or favor. I am a better woman because of you. I ask you to cover my family and all of those I am connected to. I pray that the people who do not truly love me stay from around me or be removed. I want to be around positivity and growth. I want to be that person of positivity as well for others. I also want you to mend Chanel's relationship with her dad. I want her to know she is loved. Work through my child, Lord, so she doesn't look for surprises, but for time with him. God, last night I failed miserably. I ate so many potatoes last night and drank. I must do a lot of working out today. Give me strength. In Jesus name, Amen.

February 8, 2021

Prayer: Dear God, last night my child's father didn't bring Chanel home knowing she has school. I had to pick her up because he refused to take her to school. I'm tired of arguing or trying to make him understand. As a single mom this is so stressful having to deal with his madness. Sometimes I wish I left him alone before Chanel became so aware. So, she couldn't miss what she never had. I should have never got back involved. He is flat out inconsiderate. He really does not care how I am doing mentally. He thinks being just a mom is easy. God, work through us so we can at least co-parent. In Jesus name,

Amen.

February 9, 2021

Prayer: Dear God, today I got up late, but I am so grateful that you opened my eyes at 4 am. I know that was only you. I, nor my child was feeling well today. I hope she is not sick. God, heal us. Remove anything that doesn't belong from our bodies. I'm still going to work today. I can't let being "not okay" keep me from doing what I set out to do. God, continue working through me so that I'm able to still be used by you and speak of you. Things are good, God, because of you. I am thankful for another 24 hours to see the people who love me. In Jesus name, Amen.

February 10, 2021

Prayer: Dear God, I come to you today with a grateful heart. You've done so much for and through me. I ask that you forgive me for not always being aligned and for being stubborn. I am so thankful you never gave up on me even when I wanted to give up on myself. I love the fact I can be alone and content. Even though my hormones act crazy, I have self-control, Lord. I pray that I finish this school stuff before April. I ask that you give me strength to carry out this commitment. I love you! Please watch over my family and those that love for real. Special prayer request for those that are suffering, sick, or mislead. In Jesus name, Amen.

1 Samuel 18 1-12

Joseph Coaker Notes

The moment never announces itself. Be okay with mundane tasks. One moment can change your whole life. Don't let bad choices, or people keep you from walking in your moment. What God designed collides with what man has developed. You will no longer be invited to places. You can't go back to what or whom you are related to. Don't let your need of acceptance keep you from your purpose. When moving forward, be able to take off your belt and robe, also known as the things that hold you together. You will be stripped going into your purpose.

February 15, 2021

Prayer: Dear God, I come to you for direction and instruction. I am contemplating on going to a job fair the 25th and I am coming to you for confirmation if that is something I should do. I am trying so hard to finish school online. God, give me the strength I am lacking in the thing I once started with so much joy. I must stay strong. I must keep moving forward. I am so thankful for purpose, family, understanding, and love. God, thank you for never letting your hands off me. I promise to keep following your light. In Jesus name, Amen.

Advice From Vonyae

"Keep your identity small. Don't let one belief define you. When you spend your life defining yourself in one way and that disappears, **who** will you be? Keep important aspects of your identity even if your role changes."

February 22, 2021

Prayer: Dear God, I haven't written you in a while. I've been feeling better and living better. I haven't received unemployment nor pandemic assistance since the end of January. I don't know how we are maintaining. Well, I do, all YOU. Thank you! I am so proud of myself for being consistent and loving me through this journey. I pray that never fades. I pray that everything I touch and connect with becomes blessed. It is a process to be someone God needs to lead. I truly feel "Purposeful Sisters" will be huge. I can feel it. God, continue working through me. I love you.

Thank you for Chanel's life. I pray I can live long enough to witness her grow into the woman I know she will be. P.s. God, watch over my friends, bless the things they do not discuss aloud. May it be heard by you and healed. In Jesus name, Amen.

February 23, 2021

Prayer: Dear God, what is going on in the world? People are constantly killing. We need you. I will continue to show more of you and less of me. Please watch over my connections. It is not safe in my complex. In Jesus name, Amen.

February 26, 2021

Prayer: Dear God, thank you for life. I am so grateful for the blessing you shower me in daily. To be Chanel's mom is truly a gift. I know she comes from you. She has the best parts of me and her dad. She sees things clearly. She has been here before. I've had a weird couple of days. God, continue to work through me. In Jesus name, Amen.

February 28, 2021

Prayer: Dear God, I'm tired of trying, struggling, and doing everything on my own. I can't wait to be in position. I'm thankful though. I know my day is coming. I'm focused on you, Lord. God, I am asking you to keep me close and remove all unwanted energy. In Jesus name, Amen.

March 2, 2021

Prayer: Dear God, I come to you today to thank you for giving me a boost of energy yesterday. I feel so much better. Today's sermon was titled "Model Home", and it was such a good word. I want you, God, to continue working on me and how I love my child's father because Chanel deserves peace and love from both sides. God, keep your hands on my family. I see what you are doing with me. I am breaking generational curses. Today, I will talk to Chanel in more detail that her parents' relationship is strictly to care for her. God, speak through me in that conversation with her.

Thank you, God, for giving me all that you have, haven't, and will. In Jesus name, Amen.

March 3, 2021

Prayer: Dear God, my heart is full. Thank you for all that you do. My obedience to you does not even feel like labor nor do I have to think twice. God, thank you for allowing me to be a friend this season. It is so nice to see Saudi and know her children get to experience fathership. God, continue to keep them close and work through them all. Today, I ask you, Lord, to keep me focused on school completion. In Jesus Name, Amen.

March 5, 2021

Prayer: Dear God, thank you for allowing me to go through all that I have without losing sight on who you are. You are King of all kings. The all-knowing. My true love. I pray that I stay focused on you and my purpose. I noticed my friends are even growing towards you. I see what you are doing, Lord. In Jesus name, Amen.

March 7, 2021

Prayer: Dear God, I had a real conversation with my little sister. She told me she doesn't trust me. I am not hurt nor surprised. I'm thankful for our growth and acceptance in this season. We are learning who we truly are. I am so thankful for life, love, and family. God, continue to use me. I am a vessel. Continue to work through me. In Jesus name, Amen.

March 8, 2021

Prayer: Dear God, I am so thankful for life and to be of service of the people I love and who love me. I ask that you use me fully today and forward. Continue working through me, Lord. I see what you are doing in my life, and I am grateful. In Jesus name, Amen.

March 15, 2021

Prayer: Dear God, I am so thankful for purpose, life, and the few you have around me in this season. I am grateful and my heart is full. I am so blessed to be able in this season. I know it is many who are struggling to survive, but God! I know who I am and whose I am. So, this too shall. I love you, God. I ask that you continue to work through me and Jerry. So, we can continue to communicate effectively. I praise you! Protect, lead, and love those I am connected to by blood, or other. Cover them all. God, I see what it feels like to be following you and being deeply in love with you. True happiness! I ask that you keep me from little boys and align me with my husband. In Jesus name, Amen.

March 21, 2021

Prayer: Dear God, today I pushed myself to get out of the bed to go to the cycle bar. My sister even joined me. She barely made it, but she did it! For her to show up in my world means a lot. I went to my parent's home and gave them some groceries. I love my parents. I am so blessed to be rooted in God's soil. I pray that you continue to use me fully. I love this change in me. I love who I am becoming. Keep working through me, Lord. Thank you for providing me with another 24 to be a mom and fulfill your purpose for me. In Jesus name, Amen.

<u>March 25, 2021</u>

Prayer: Dear God, I'm tired. I must keep going for my daughter. I'm done spending. I need to be saving. God, be my accountant. Keep me focused. Protect us from evil and harm. In Jesus name, Amen.

March 31, 2021

Prayer: God, wow! I am so grateful for life and purpose. Continue to use me as a vessel. I see what you are doing in me. I have better relationships with those I love. I appreciate them deeper and have a clearer understanding of my calling. I pray that I continue to see you and only you. I pray that I master consistency to your vision for my life. I am working hard on being my best self to achieve many things through my family. In Jesus name, Amen.

April 3,2021

Prayer: Dear God, I want to thank you for all you've done for my family and self. Today, I come to you with vision. I want to create a union of some sort. I ask that you lead me and work through me on this. God, continue to work through those around me. In Jesus name, Amen.

<u>April 5, 2021</u>

Prayer: Good morning, God! I hear you clearly and see you more clearly than ever. It amazes me, not frightens me. Only you can do what you do in my life. I ask that you keep my connections protected and myself. Today, I invited Que cycling; I'm excited. Chapter #28 is approaching! This year, I'll never forget because I gave Jesus my "yes"! Thank you for another 24 hours to get it right. In Jesus name, Amen.

April 6, 2021

Prayer: Dear God, I come to you with uncertainty. I want to finish this medical program, but I also want to be available for my daughter this summer. God, guide me. Lead me! Move my feet in the direction you want me to go. I got this! I do! I can! Sticking to the goal. I love you! Grateful for another 24 hours. In Jesus name, Amen.

April 10, 2021

Prayer: Dear God, I come to you today with a grateful heart. I am so blessed and happy. Continue to work through me and others I am connected to. My birthday this year was amazing from start to finish. I am so excited about being back in the church tomorrow. God, I see you more than ever now. Thank you for another 24 hours. In Jesus name, Amen.

April 11, 2021

Pastor Daryl Arnold Sermon Notes

God has revealed to you who he really is. The father has matured you. Stop giving people access to your life that has not matured. Keys: Righteousness, peace, and joy. It went from what you heard to what you know. I know I've changed. Simon's name was changed to Peter. Transformation! You are now spiritually matured so now you have the keys. God does not want you annoyed; He wants you anointed. - Matthew 16:19.

April 12, 2021

Prayer: Dear God, I hear you loud and clear. I am working for the people. May my connections be protected and blessed. Thank you again for another 24 hours. In Jesus name, Amen.

April 14, 2021

SJR LIVE On Instagram "Get Up and Do" Notes

God will give you strength in your inadequacy. Live in your inadequacy. Bringing change, I am partnering with Jesus. I cannot do this on my own. My weakness plus God's strength is having a collision. The revolution is in your vulnerability. Take inventory from that place. I'm hungry for something bigger than me. What can I produce with what I got? Give what you got.

Job 14:1 and John 16:33

Your excuses just gave someone else an opportunity.

April 18, 2021

Prayer: Dear God, today I got baptized!! My dad didn't allow my mom to come. Just as he didn't allow her to attend my high school graduation. I'm not upset. God, you are my father! Thank you, Jesus! I was so happy to see my friend Que, daughter, and sister! In Jesus name, Amen.

April 19, 2021

Dear God, it is the day after giving my "yes" publicly and I feel new. I am so thankful for what I have now. I know my purpose. I am so grateful to be walking in. This journal has helped me process and be okay with my mess because in my mess there is always a message. Thank you, Lord, for what you are doing in my life. In Jesus name, Amen.

April 26, 2021

Prayer: Dear God, thank you. I really enjoyed my weekend with my little sister. We needed that understanding. Continue to show me how to be a better believer by understanding what I don't and digging deeper into what I do. I am praying for my child's father due to the revelation I had the other day. Please cover him. Thank you for everything you've done for me and will do. We are up next! In Jesus name, Amen.

<u>May 3, 2021</u>

Prayer: Dear God, I come to you today with so much thanks. You've answered my prayers. So thankful for life and the ones I have in my life. In Jesus name, Amen.

<u>May 4, 2021</u>

Prayer: Dear God, I had sex today, Lord, with a close friend. I don't have much to say but forgive me father. Today he turns himself in. My emotions won. Forgive me father. In Jesus name, Amen.

May 7, 2021

Prayer: Dear God, I come to you today with so much sadness for my grandmother Lilly. She passed away this morning. I will miss her deeply, but she saved me to save the others. Thank you, God, for allowing me to experience a true woman of God. Until next time. I love you! Thank you, Jesus. In Jesus name, Amen.

May 16, 2021

Prayer: Dear God, today I went to the morning service at 9:30 at church because later today I'll be burying my grandmother. Keep me covered, Lord. In Jesus name, Amen.

Pastor Daryl Arnold Sermon Notes

Where you can't feel my presence remember my promises. How to deal with divine disappointments. God will never lie, limit, or leave you.

How on time was that word? Thank you, Jesus!

<u>May 17, 2021</u>

Prayer: Dear God, today I started fasting. I am excited to see, feel, hear, and know what you have in store. I want what you have for me. I want you to show me what I've been overlooking and missing on this journey. I am so thankful for life and vision. May you continue working on and through me. Also, through my connections. I am fasting until I receive clarity and a breakthrough. In Jesus name, Amen.

May 20, 2021

Day 5 Of Fasting

Prayer: Dear God, today I renew my lease. UGH! I didn't want to, but I know you want me to sit still. So, I am. I plan on passing the board exam and going back to work in September. I am excited. I want to make my own schedule or work only part time. I am so thankful you trust me, Lord, to mother Chanel. So grateful for life and love. God, please continue to work through me. I love you! Thank you for another 24 hours. In Jesus name, Amen.

<u>May 23, 2021</u>

Prayer: Dear God, thank you for waking me this morning. I am so grateful for everything you've done and are doing for me and my connections. I am most happy with the divine connections you brought into my life. The things I see, feel, and know now are only because of you. Thank you for trusting me. I appreciate everything you've done for me. I ask that you continue to work through. Less of me and more of you. I still feel my grandmother's presence and believe it or not my dad does too. Today, baby Ary gets Christened. Such a blessing! Today, I wrote my friend in jail. Align my heart and mind to agree with your plans for my life. In Jesus name, Amen.

<u>May 24, 2021</u>

Prayer: Dear God, thank you for waking me up this morning. I am so grateful for life and love. My mom seems so uneasy today. Grant her peace. I know losing her mother must be hard. Please help and heal her, Lord. God continue working through me. In Jesus name, Amen.

May 25, 2021

Prayer: Dear God, I come to you today to say thank you for everything you've done and are doing. I really do care for my guy friend. He really cares about me. He's always been in my corner, but since we've had sex, and he is incarcerated, I see him differently. God, if it's not for me, please give me a sign. I know I already had sex with him, but I won't ever again. Give me a clear sign I can't ignore because I don't want to date anything not from you. My plan this weekend is to see my friends and their kids. I'm so excited! God, continue working through me. In Jesus name, Amen.

May 26, 2021

Prayer: Dear God, I am working hard to bring this vision to life. I know this is only from you. By how clear it is. I am so thankful for purpose and mothership. I don't take any of this for granted. Being that I was able to give birth due to my circumstances. All you! Now I know why PCOS had to occur because you want me to give birth to your visions for humanity. I plan on taking the business class in September. We shall see! In Jesus name, Amen.

May 28, 2021

Prayer: Dear God, thank you for waking me up this morning. Today, I'm going to visit my friends. I am so grateful. I'm praying for cautious drivers. Prayers for my Paul as well; keep him covered, God. Keep my uncle Tony in line. His dad needs him more than ever now. In Jesus name, Amen.

June 1, 2021

Prayer: Dear God, thank you for another 24 hours to do life with you and for you. My mom is thirsty for you and so is my dad. I know I stepped out of turn, God, but my dad is so nasty towards my mom. I know he doesn't know what he does. Heal them inside and out, Lord. I can't believe I asked for a quality guy friend, and you sent my friend of 10 years back into my life. The way he cares is different than what I am used to. It is refreshing. God, thank you! God, I ask that you continue to work through me and my connections. Thank you and my angels for keeping us safe. In Jesus name, Amen.

June 2, 2021

Prayer: Dear God, I am a few pages done with reading book #2. So excited to start *Women Evolve*. God, I thank you for life and love. God, grant me clarity on my purpose with him. I should have kept it platonic until I received your full direction. He values my daughter. Always has. Is he the one? I will listen closely to you for the answer because I don't want to continue leading this man on if he is not from you. I trust you, God, with my entire life. Thank you! In Jesus name, Amen.

June 3, 2021

Prayer: Dear God, today a cat ran into my house. I know it was a message from you. Thank you! God, I am so thankful for you saving me. I am so hopeful and full of love because of you. Thank you. I'll never thirst again. You filled me up. You made me whole. You work in mysterious ways. Next month unemployment ends, but you sent my sister to move in and pay rent. God, thank you! I needed help. I see you! I hear you! God, I ask that you cover my sister and protect my sister from her own emotions. Build us up, Lord! Thank you for another 24 hours. In Jesus name, Amen.

June 6, 2021

Prayer: Dear God, I come to you today with gratitude for vision and courage. Today's word was divine and profound. I am so grateful and full for the opportunity I created today. It was so on time. The fact the youth minister's wife had a look of belief in my vision makes me hopeful. I am so ready to serve you and your kingdom. I'm ready to work for you on the frontline. God, I ask that you continue to work through me and my connections. I see exactly what you are doing, and I trust you with my entire life. Thank you! In Jesus name, Amen.

<u>June 7, 2021</u>

Prayer: Dear God, I come to you with a grateful heart and understanding spirit. Today, I prayed for my friend Que and reminded her how good you truly are. But in order to see and experience your favor and excellence we must believe and be faithful. God, I haven't had a period in a long time. Will I be able to have another child if I was to want one? I always said I didn't want another one, but you know what I need, and don't. For now, I'll pray for my health and delivering this purpose and vision to my church. I know you have something big in store for my life; I can feel it. Thank you for trusting me. I ask that you bless my connections and keep harm and evil away from me and my loved ones. In Jesus name, Amen.

June 9, 2021

Prayer: Dear God, thank you for waking me up this morning. I am so grateful for life and love. God, please keep me covered and my connections. I am so thankful for peace with my child's father. God, I ask that whatever my consequence may be for having sex in May that I can live with it. I have forgiven myself as you've forgiven me. I haven't been feeling well. I want to get back into the gym or cycle. I need to be easy on myself. Watch over him while in prison. Show him YOU! Make it plain and clear to him, Lord. Show your face. Today, my sister and I are filming for the podcast. Thank you! In Jesus name, Amen.

June 10, 2021

Prayer: Dear God, thank you for everything. I mean the divine connections, opportunities, and the support. I feel so weak today in my friendships. IDK! I need to take a break from the world for a while. God, also thank you for deliverance from the devil and depression. So, blessed! Continue to use me and work through me. I love you! In Jesus name, Amen.

June 12, 2021

Prayer: Dear God, thank you for understanding and love. I appreciate everything you are doing in my life and for my connections. I ask that you cover my sister and mother so that they can have a healthy relationship. Also, I ask that you watch over the people I trust that pretend to care about me. I am so thankful for the friendship I have within my sistership with Sarah. God, I am so excited about the business. Continue using me and working through me. Thankful for another 24 hours. In Jesus name, Amen.

June 14, 2021

Prayer: Dear God, thank you for waking me to be a mother, friend, daughter, and servant. God, are you showing me he is not the one? Make it plain. I'm so thankful for our relationship. You've helped me so much. Thank you for keeping me close. God, continue working through my connections. So, blessed! In Jesus name, Amen.

June 15, 2021

Prayer: Dear God, I come to you with deep gratitude. I've been extremely tired. I pray that my health is intact. I ask you for supernatural energy today. I need energy to wake up ready to serve. I've been slacking, so I feel. I moved out of your will, and I am beginning to feel a weakened spirit. God, I don't want anything or anyone that is not from you. God, I miss my granny so much. I'm not the same. I feel weak. God, help me. I need strength to eat, drink water, and BE. Today is good, but I ask that you pour into me so it can be great. Continue to watch over my connections. Thank you! In Jesus name, Amen.

June 18, 2021

Prayer: Dear God, thank you for waking me and my daughter today. Another day to fulfill your purpose. I am so grateful for my connections and love. It is an honor to be of service to the people who love me. God, continue working through me and on my parents, they need you desperately. I don't think I'm going to ATL. I have no desire to. I would miss church. I can't spiritually miss service nor an opportunity to speak with the youth minister about my kingdom vision. God, I ask that you watch over him while he does his time. Also, work through him. He needs you and he is going to have to choose you before he can walk with me. I love you, God! In Jesus name, Amen.

June 20, 2021

Prayer: Dear God, thank you for being patient with me. Thank you for not allowing myself to get drunk. I had a good time, it was needed. I was able to love on a friend and dance. God, protect DeeDee! Reveal her true intentions, Lord! God, it is truly beautiful hearing me speak about wellness and gratitude. She thinks it's her, but she'll soon learn it is all YOU! Make me an example to lead my connections to you. God, I love you. In Jesus name, Amen.

June 23, 2021

Prayer: Dear God, I have been feeling uneasy here lately. Tired and weary. God, cleanse my mind, body, and soul. I need you desperately, God. I ask that you continue to cover my connections. Thank you for everything you've done, doing, and will do. I appreciate the holy spirit and his guidance and discernment. I trust you with my whole life, entirely. Thank you for direction. I ask that you continue to work on my guy friend so that he becomes a better human than he already is. I rushed over to my mom's house to pray for and over her. I see what you are doing, Lord. In Jesus name, Amen.

June 25, 2021

Prayer: Dear God, I come to you today asking for protection, correction, and love. I've been protecting my child's father's feelings and not caring about my guy friend's. God, allow him to see my heart. I really do care. My sister moved in with me. I love having her here. I love our talks and honesty. God, continue to work through us individually. We did our introduction today for Purposeful Sisters. Working our purpose! God, I don't trust DeeDee. Continue to reveal her true intentions in dreams. Thank you for life! Keep

your hands on my child's father,
please. In Jesus name, Amen.

June 28, 2021

Prayer: Dear God, I come to you today asking that you continue working through me. I ask that as I fulfill your plans, you grant my sister and I clarity on this journey. May we never lose focus or sight on you, or our purpose. I am so thankful for life, growth, and healing. I am in so much because of you. Thank you! Being able to witness my child grow and discover her truth is so beautiful and pure. God, I let go of Domo. I ask that you cover him and continue working on me and my future husband. Thank you, Jesus. In your mighty name, Amen.

June 30, 2021

Prayer: Dear God, thank you for waking my daughter and I up. Yesterday she had a rough day. I ask that whatever is hurting or bothering my daughter comes to surface in a manner we can heal and discuss. I don't want her to hold it in or explode. God, I am grateful for my now. I ask that you cover my family, friends, and connections. Continue to work through me, Lord, so they see and only see you, Lord. Protect us from evil. And hold my parents close. They desperately need you. Thank you for all you've done, are doing, and will do. Love you. In Jesus name, Amen.

July 1, 2021

Prayer: Dear God, I come to you today with a hopeful spirit for my connections to seek you. Thank you, God, for everything you've done and will do. I am so grateful you kept me close. [10:30pm] Dear God, I am coming to you about my little sister's selfish spirit. Today, I was bothered by the comment she made today. I pray that she experiences conviction about her behavior and how she is taking advantage of me only hurts her. God, I could speak on it with her, but I want you to work on her spirit personally before we have a conversation. So, God, I ask you to work on her and through her. I see you, God. Thank you, in Jesus's name, Amen.

July 8, 2021

Prayer: Dear God, thank you for gracing me with life and abundance of love. God, I don't take a second for granted being a mother, daughter, and sister. Today, I am so tired, my body is exhausted. PCOS is making me so tired no matter what I eat or do. I need to be studying for my exam, but I haven't been in it. God, grant me strength and out of this spirit of CAN'T DO. God, I've been sharing the gospel, but not praying as much as I need to do. God, I need you to cover me fully and work through me. In Jesus name, Amen.

July 11, 2021

Dear God, I come to you today with a calm spirit and hopeful heart that my person finds you, before me. God, I need help. I need a job that brings me peace and great benefits. God, order my steps please. I desire to be off on Tuesdays and Sundays. I need to make more time to study for my boards. I just don't have the motivation. Help me! I need to refocus. It seems as if my mind is everywhere. God, give me strength!

July 12, 2021

Dear God, thank you for my blessings today. Today was good. I am grateful. I pray I find a job that works for my life. God, lead me. I'm going to stop saying, "I trust." Yet, still touching what I give to you. Forgive father. I love you!

<u>July 15, 2021</u>

Dear God, I come to you with deep gratitude. I've been extremely tired. I think I am sick. I pray that my health is intact. I ask for supernatural energy. I spoke too soon to Domo or did I, Lord? God I don't want anything or anyone that is not from you. God, I miss my granny so much. I'm not the same. I feel weak. God help me! I need strength to just BE these days. Lord, please watch over my connections.

July 16, 2021

Dear God, thank you for another day to love and share the gospel. I feel alot better now. God, continue to heal me. I have an interview today, Lord. God, I ask that you go before me and if it is for me, may your will be done. God, thank you for trusting me with life. Sex is not worth losing connection with you.

July 21, 2021

Dear God, thank you for the career opportunity at LSI. I am so grateful. I ask that you continue to work through me. God, I'm frustrated because for 8 weeks I need someone to take my child to gymnastics. She's worked too hard for me to take her out because of my work schedule. God, lead me to make the right decision. I wish her dad would be my teammate right now. I need help. God, I ask that you grant him a career that works for him. God, help us to make the best decisions for our child. I'll help him, Lord, but you must help me, Lord. Don't give up on him, Lord. He needs you. We need you.

July 23, 2021

Dear God, thank you for today for life. I am so grateful. I ask that you cover my family and connections. I ask that you work in my friend Derrian's heart so that she can see all of your goodness and see that she is worthy. I love you, God. I enjoyed doing ministry work today with my daughter. It was really nice. Lord, continue working on me and through me, Lord.

August 5, 2021

Dear God, forgive me for neglecting you. I'm here. God, continue to work on me and through me. I miss you so much. I've been thinking unclean thoughts. Lord, purify my mind. God watch over Domo as he does his time in jail.

August 6, 2021

Dear God, thank you for another day of life. I am so grateful. I ask that you continue to cover my life and my connections. I ask, God, that you continue to work on and through me. God, I need you to keep me away from having a lonely spirit. I want to be consumed in you and in love with you entirely. I ask that you forgive me for all my sins and grant me wisdom and understanding.

August 13, 2021

Dear God, thank you for life and purpose. I am so grateful my daughter completed her first week of school. She is enjoying every bit of it. Continue to use her for your glory and protect her heart. God thank you for Chanel's village. They are helping me and I am learning how to accept help because I can't do this by myself. God, continue to process me. I need your spirit. God, cover my finances. Teach me how to steward my finances well. God, keep working on my mom and sister please. They need you. No matter how healed my sister says she is, I know she is hurting. Heal my family, Lord.

August 17, 2021

Dear God, I thank you for using me to fufill your purpose. God, I ask that you continue working through me. I am so grateful for employment. God, thank you for your mercy and grace. You kept me. God, I ask that IF this apartment does not come available November or December that I am able to apply for Habitat Housing. I ask that you keep me focused on YOU. There is alot going on in the world. May I not get lost in emotion and conform, but be inspired to do more. God, thank you for all that you have done, doing, and will do. I love you!

August 19, 2021

Dear God, I come to you today with an open heart. I am so thankful for life. I ask that you cover and heal me, Lord. Heal my sister, Lord. She needs you. God, continue working through me. God, I am praying for my husband; that when he arrives, I am prepared for him. Keep working on me. May I never be ungrateful. May I always be full of love and thanksgiving. God, provide me with the skills and knowledge to do this job correctly.

August 23, 2021

Dear God, I come to you thankful that I didn't give into smoking. You are delivering me. I see you working. I rebuke anything not of you or from you in Jesus name. I pray that I continue to do your will. I will serve you, Lord, and your people for the rest of my days. I will stay focused on you. I ask that you forgive me for all of my sins. I am thankful for another day of life to love.

August 25, 2021

Dear God, I come to you today with a grateful heart and a full spirit. You woke me up another day to love and share your gospel. Thank you! God, I don't ask for anything, but your love, Father. You are my dad. My go-to friend. I am learning to trust your plan fully. I catch myself wanting a man which know I am not ready for. So, God, continue to work through me. I love Domo, but I am not in love with him. I am interested in the man I don't have to tell to not disrespect me. God, cover me from evil. Protect my child from bullies and evil do-ers. Also, Lord, I pray for Tristen's health. That you will heal him inside and out. Thank you in advance.

August 26, 2021

Dear God, I just found out I have herpes yesterday. I haven't had sex in three months. How is this so? Is that why I've been so fatigued?! I am in shock, but I am thankful for answered prayers when it comes to my health. I knew he was not the one, but thank you for the confirmation. I played with my anointing and burned myself for good. God, I ask that you heal me so my spirit aligns with you. May I be made whole and like you. God, I still desire to be loved properly. I desire to be desired and loved properly. I deserve a great Godly man. I do. I believe. I have faith. I am not less than. I am more than because of YOU.

September 6, 2021

Dear God, I stopped smoking. I realized I'm hurting and only masking my issues. God, I feel like I am back at square one with my emotions. I feel everything. I don't know why I can't even be a decent mother. I feel like I am always yelling and crying. She doesn't even listen to me anymore. I need your help, God. I've lost so much. I need your help recovering my peace. I don't trust anybody and I don't want to. Help me! I feel like giving up. I need guidance, support, and love to provide for my child. I am losing it. I feel as if I have nothing to give.

September 9, 2021

Dear God, I come to you so grateful and full for the job I have. They are so understanding and I am so blessed to be able to say that. My family is healthy and I am well. May you continue to work through me. Lead and guide me, Lord. I ask that you keep the enemy from me. I am grateful to be able to exemplify your works. I love you, Lord. Keep using my friend Que, Lord.

September 10, 2021

Dear God, thank you for carrying me through this training class. I am so blessed for the opportunity. I will continue working hard and giving my best at all that I do. Thank you for loving, caring, and guiding me through it all. I will stay focused on you and only you. Continue working through my family and friends. We need you. Asking that you heal my bloodline, Lord.

<u>September 13, 2021</u>

Dear God, I come to you today so grateful that I am able to provide and love my daughter fully. I ask that you continue to work through me. May I remain in your will for my life. I will continue to share my testimony and the good news to bring people to you, Lord. You gave me a life more abundantly. Thank you. I am so thankful for the people who genuinely love me. Thank you, Jesus, for paying the ultimate price for my sins. Lord, be with my child's father, he yearns to be loved. Shower him with your love.

September 17, 2021

Dear God, thank you for allowing me to see another day. Continue to use me, Lord, that I may touch your people and bring them closer to you. May today be great!

<u>September 22, 2021</u>

Dear God, thank you for another day of being a friend, daughter, sister, and mother. I am so grateful for life and love. I don't feel good, Lord. Lord keep my child that is all I ask

September 25, 2021

Dear God, I miss you, Lord. My habits are poor. I fell off, but I still desire your presence. Thank you for my job, village, and loved ones. I am working hard to be my best self and being my best self and being financially stable. I ask that you cover my connections. I love you, God. I don't take anything for granted. I pray that Sheena is still alive. Lord, just allow her family and loved ones to know she is not suffering at least. Grant me wisdom, Lord, in this season. May everyday I show people you through my life.

September 26, 2021

Dear God, I come to you thankful and full. God, continue to work through me. May people witness my life and be convicted to change and draw closer to you. I ask that you perform the supernatural in my life. I am in need of a miracle. A shift. God, I am a lover. I desire to have a husband, God. But if you only have called me to love you and your people then that is what I will do. May I never outgrow my position as a servant or weary in doing good.

October 14, 2021

Dear God, thank you for helping me see things clearly. God, I see clearer now that you wanted certain relationships broken. It is some things, God, you didn't fix because you never meant it to be a part of me. Thank you for seeing the full picture. I release it all to you. I give up trying to do it for you without you. Teach me how to remain in you, Lord.

June 9, 2022

Am I even qualified?
I was not a person who willingly walked into purpose, or with God even. It took trials, tribulations, and Judas to get me here.

Last year, I got baptized on April 18, 2021 and exactly a MONTH later fell short of God's way of living. I couldn't forgive myself. Make matters worse, two days later my granny passed away. Between doing CPR on my grandmother and praying with my mother head to head for a stronger heartbeat. God forgave me. He even reminded me of my assignment, my purpose, that I still had that I thought I lost due to falling short. I got up that same day with forgiveness to carry on what God called me to do. Three months later, I got a call back that I was diagnosed with HSV1. Just when I thought I overcame falling short, God REMINDS me IT COST BIG to fall short because my assignment is not just FOR ME – it is about the souls connected to me. I felt unworthy of his plans for me. I felt unqualified to push the gospel with a stain on my life. BUT! Somewhere between me answering every call from God and interceding for others, God healed me.

I struggled deep with how I am going to forgive the man who has been my "friend" for 13+ years. I asked God questions like:

How is it that the man I made to wait for 13 years robs me of my entire intimacy? He answered: The devil patrols the earth waiting patiently to devour you.

How did I not see it coming? He answered: You did. You prayed before the encounter. You ignored me.

Why would he betray me? He answered: Why would you betray me?

Why would he lie to me? He answered: Why would you believe man after knowing MY truth.

God revealed to me HE was only my Judas - the BETRAYAL was necessary.

Yesterday during bible study, God spoke to me in scripture Jeremiah 1:12. The Lord said, "That's right, and it means that I am watching, and I will certainly carry out all my plans." Meaning HE SEES ALL, AND STILL HE PLANS TO CARRY OUT HIS PURPOSE THROUGH ME.

June 29, 2022

Called OUT!

I didn't understand why people would rather conform to a title, rather than simply just be. I questioned, "Why do people feel empowered to live up to being a leader, rather than just being a leader?" I didn't have an answer until I witnessed Sarah Jakes Roberts LIVE in Nashville.

See, I ran from big verbs, big titles, and big relationships because my PAST identity was always UNCERTAIN and UNSURE. I was not afraid of failing. I was afraid of accepting who I was becoming in Christ. I was always a person who would go into rooms naturally just 'being'. I want to point out that not accepting a title of WHO YOU ARE OR WHOSE YOU ARE will allow space for the enemy to use you.

Once you accept your titles – you accept the job description – than you perform according to the titles you've accepted. That's how you create CLEAR [Boundaries].

As a child, I always heard negative things from my biological father that stained my outlook on how I viewed myself. That is why it has been difficult for me to accept titles, compliments, awards, rewards, and gifts.

People would meet me ONCE and compliment my character as if they'd never met a genuine, or authentic person before. It concerned me until I realized it is not ME they are seeing – IT IS GOD!

But! After being a witness of Pastor Sarah, I realized I was always being picked on and pointed out because God has been calling me out my entire life. I never felt bigger, better, or used my God given power because I never accepted FULLY who God designed me to be.

Know the difference between humility; a low view of one's own importance and doubtful; feeling of uncertainty. WE ARE ENOUGH, WE ARE BIG, WE ARE SO MUCH more than WE allow OURSELVES to accept. TOGETHER LET'S ACCEPT OUR POWER!

My God is not small so neither are WE!

Accept the calling or continue being called out!

How’s it going.

ARISE Michelle!

I’ve accepted I cannot outrun or outwit God. I surrender completely. My soul says, “Yes”. I have wrestled long enough. Truth is, I can’t lie. I wish I did this sooner because this is true freedom. I can’t mask what God never intended to cover up. I thank God that He met me where I was and shaped me into who He always knew. My purpose was never a place, but a state of becoming who I’ve always been in Christ. I am found!

About The Author

Michelle Howell is a passionate philanthropist, and the founder of a nonprofit organization dedicated to creating purposeful relationships. With a deep commitment to community service, she has dedicated her career to addressing critical social issues and empowering individuals through impactful initiatives. As a devoted mother and daughter, Michelle draws inspiration from her personal experiences to drive her work, ensuring that her efforts positively influence the lives of others. Her leadership, compassion, and vision continue to shape the future of her organization and the communities she serves.

www.ingramcontent.com/pod-product-compliance
Lightning Source LLC
La Vergne TN
LVHW020627100826
845148LV00012B/2074